ECHOES of HOPE

Mapping Your Path With 100 Empowering Words

While every precaution has been taken in the preparation of this book, the publisher assumes no responsibility for errors or omissions, or for damages resulting from the use of the information contained herein.

ECHOES OF HOPE

First edition. March 12, 2024.

Copyright © 2024 Tylor Miller.

ISBN: 979-8224475216

Written by Tylor Miller.

VOLUME ONE

ECHOES of HOPE

Mapping Your Path With
100 Empowering Words

Tylor

Jordon

Miller

<u>Echoes of Hope</u>

THIS BOOK IS A DEDICATION to my close family who has supported me through every phase of my life. Angella, Gloria, O'Shea, Odaine, and Earl, thank you for everything. I have been stereotyped and doubted all my life, nevertheless, you all believed in me. This book is a dedication to you.

Introduction

Welcome to "Echoes of Hope," a sacred journey into the power of affirmation, where each word on these pages reverberates like a prayer, inviting you to embrace the dance of life. In this exploration called "life," we know that things may not always seem ideal and perfect. But with these prayers, let us shift our minds towards good, and embrace each imperfection.

As we step into this dance, we recognize the echoes of hope that resound through the tapestry of our lives. Our affirmations become more than words; they become heartfelt whispers, resonating in the sanctuary of our hearts, reaching out to the Lord for strength. It is an acknowledgment that our journey, with all its twists and turns, is a part of our development—a design that includes our aspirations, challenges, and triumphs into a harmonious melody guided by Jesus.

Each affirmation is a testament to the belief that we matter. We find strength in our trials, joy in our blessings, and purpose in our journey.

So, dear reader, as you immerse yourself in the echoes of hope within these pages, may you feel love in every word. May you recognize that you are not alone on this journey, because God is with you, guiding your steps and infusing each moment with purpose.

Motivation

TAKE A MOMENT TO SIT back and reflect on your life...
What would it be like if we only did things we were motivated
to do?

Motivation is like a sudden spark. Intense and heartfelt,
but not always dependable. While it can truly fuel our passion
and lead us toward our goals, there can be times when
motivation diminishes, leaving us feeling jammed. However,
we must understand that motivation is just one part of the
equation.

Discipline, on the other hand, is the commitment to showing up consistently, putting in the work, and clinging to the plan or routine, even when motivation diminishes. Combining motivation with discipline creates a powerful harmony, increasing the likelihood of sustained success.

Motivation + Discipline = Sustained Success

<u>Resilience</u>

RE·SIL·IENCE

/rəˈzilēəns/

noun

1.

the capacity to withstand or to recover from difficulties; toughness.

Challenges may come. They are inevitable. We cannot control whatever difficulties that happen around us, but we can control how we respond to them. Therefore, let us all emphasize that resilience is not about avoiding challenges, but about navigating through them.

So, say it with me....

"I am resilient in the face of challenges, and I grow stronger with each obstacle."

Fall seven times, stand up eight.

<u>Success</u>

As you dance through challenges and savor triumphs, let success be the soundtrack that fuels your passion and resilience. Your unique melody of success is a masterpiece in the making.

Achieving success is not just about reaching the destination; it is about the journey, the lessons learned, and the growth experienced along the way. Success is the sweet result of persistent effort, resilience in the face of challenges, and the unwavering belief that you can achieve greatness.

Success: Your Symphony of Triumphs

Courage

IN THE JOURNEY OF COURAGE, vulnerability is your greatest strength. Opening your heart and embracing authenticity, you discover the courage to be yourself unapologetically. Every step forward, no matter how small, is a testament to the bravery within.

Courage is not the absence of fear but the audacity to face it head-on. Imagine courage as a lantern guiding you through the darkest nights, lighting the way to your boldest dreams.

Let courage be your anthem, a melody of fear conquered, dreams pursued, and authenticity celebrated. In the symphony of life, your courage is the resounding note that echoes long after the music fades.

If you see me fighting a bear, pray for the bear.

Determination

DETERMINATION IS YOUR turbo boost, propelling you through challenges with unstoppable force. Picture determination as the engine revving up before a race, ready to sprint toward your goals. It is the fire in your belly that turns "I can't" into "I will."

In the adventure of determination, setbacks are detours, not dead ends. Each obstacle is a chance to show your grit and prove that your spirit is unbreakable. Fuel your determination with a mix of passion and persistence and watch as you blaze a trail towards success.

So, rev up that determination engine, accelerate through obstacles, and feel the wind of accomplishment in your hair. Your journey is a thrilling ride, and determination is the turbo-charged magic that keeps you on the fast track to victory.

$$(I\ can't) - (n't) = I\ can$$

<u>Positivity</u>

For me, growing up in Miami made it challenging for me to consume positivity. But as I have grown, I learned to imagine positivity as a radiant beam that transforms challenges into opportunities and setbacks into stepping stones. It is the contagious energy that uplifts not only you but everyone around you.

In the dance of positivity, gratitude is your rhythm. Celebrate the small victories, savor the simple joys, and let your positivity dance create a symphony of good vibes. Embrace a mindset where every challenge is a chance to shine, and every setback is a setup for a greater comeback.

So, sprinkle positivity like confetti, and let your optimism be the melody of your life's soundtrack. Your positivity is a magnetic force, attracting joy, opportunities, and a cascade of good vibes.

Live life to the fullest, and focus on the positive

<u>Confidence</u>

CONFIDENCE IS THE STRUT in your step, the superhero cape you wear every day. Picture confidence not as arrogance but as a warm embrace of your worth. It is the inner cheerleader reminding you that you've got this.

In the dance of confidence, self-love is your partner. Embrace your quirks, celebrate your strengths, and let your confidence waltz through life's challenges. With every confident stride, you rewrite self-doubt into self-belief.

So, stand tall, shoulders back, and let your confidence radiate like a beacon. You are not just walking; you are strutting on the runway of your success.

Confidence is not a show; it is your soul doing the tango.

Empowerment

———●———

EMPOWERMENT IS THE ignition switch to your power. Imagine empowerment as a surge of energy, awakening the dormant potential within. It is not about control; it is about unleashing the forces that make you unstoppable.

In the journey of empowerment, knowledge is your fuel. Arm yourself with wisdom, learn from every experience, and watch as empowerment propels you to heights you never thought possible.

So, flip the switch, embrace your strength, and let empowerment be the driving force of your narrative. Your empowerment is not just a state of being, it is a revolution.

Empowerment: Your superpower in the game of life

Focus

FOCUS IS YOUR SPOTLIGHT in the chaos, illuminating the path to your goals. Picture focus as a laser beam, cutting through distractions and homing in on your priorities. It is the secret sauce that transforms dreams into reality.

In the symphony of focus, mindfulness is your conductor. Tune in to the present moment, silence the noise, and let your focus orchestrate the masterpiece of your achievements.

SO, SHARPEN YOUR FOCUS like a well-crafted arrow, aimed straight at your aspirations. Your focus is not just concentration; it is the magic wand that turns ideas into accomplishments.

Lock innnnnnnnnnnnnn!

Passion

———◉———

PASSION IS THE HEARTBEAT of your journey, the rhythm that makes life a dance. Imagine passion as a flame, burning brightly in your soul. It is the driving force that turns the regular into the extraordinary.

In the dance of passion, curiosity is your partner. Explore, discover, and let your passion be the compass that guides you through uncharted territories. With every step, let your heart lead the way.

So, let your passion blaze like a shooting star, leaving a trail of inspiration in its wake.

Your passion is not just a feeling; it is the fuel that propels you towards your dreams.

Try feeling the heartbeat of your wildest dreams. That is passion.

Perseverance

Perseverance is the marathon of your spirit, the endurance that outlasts any challenge. Picture perseverance not as a sprint but as a steady jog, pacing yourself through the highs and lows. It is the unwavering commitment to reaching the finish line.

In the adventure of perseverance, resilience is your trusty companion. Bounce back from setbacks, learn from every stumble, and let your perseverance be the anthem that plays in the background of your triumphs.

So, lace up your shoes, embrace the journey, and let perseverance be the heartbeat of your resilience. Your perseverance is not just endurance; it is the victory lap of your tenacity.

Persevere by turning every stumble into a victory dance.

Vision

VISION IS THE COMPASS guiding your journey, the map to the extraordinary. Envision your dreams, not as distant mirages, but as tangible destinations waiting to be explored. It is the panoramic view that stretches beyond the horizon, urging you to dream big.

In the symphony of vision, creativity is your muse. Paint your aspirations with vibrant hues, sculpt your goals with imagination, and let your vision be the masterpiece that unfolds one stroke at a time.

Therefore, put on the lenses of possibility, gaze into the future, and let your vision be the North Star guiding your endeavors. Your vision is not just a dream; it is the roadmap to your destiny.

Be DaViisionary. Shout out to DaArtBureau LLC.

Growth

Growth is the garden of possibilities, where every challenge is a seed of transformation. Envision growth not as a destination but as a continual bloom, each petal representing a lesson learned and every bud a promise of future potential.

In the garden of growth, adaptability is your green thumb. Embrace change, nourish your roots with new experiences, and watch as your growth becomes a vibrant testament to the ever-evolving masterpiece of your life.

So, cultivate your garden with curiosity, water it with resilience, and let growth be the fragrant bouquet that accompanies your journey. Your growth is not just progress; it is the ongoing story of your becoming.

Where challenges bloom and build into the flowers of wisdom.
(BuildBuildBuild)

Achievement

⸻ ◉ ⸻

ACHIEVEMENT IS THE trophy of your efforts, the medal that validates your journey. Picture achievement not as a one-time event but as a collection of milestones, each representing a triumph over challenges. It is tangible proof that your hard work has paid off.

In the gallery of achievement, celebration is your curator. Acknowledge your victories, big and small, savor the flavor of success, and let achievement be the gallery that displays the masterpieces of your perseverance.

So, raise your glass, applaud your journey, and let achievement be the applause echoing in the auditorium of your life. Your achievements are not just accolades; they are the chapters of your success story.

Achievement: Your story is told in triumphs.

Belief

BELIEF IS THE ANCHOR in the storm, the unwavering trust in your potential. See belief not as blind faith but as a sturdy foundation, grounding you when the winds of doubt blow. It is the confidence in your abilities that propels you forward.

In the tapestry of belief, self-affirmation is your thread. Weave positive thoughts into the fabric of your mind, strengthen your convictions, and let belief be the quilt that wraps you in the warmth of your potential.

So, stitch your dreams with confidence, patch by patch, and let belief be the cozy blanket on the couch of your aspirations. Your belief is not just a mindset; it is the comforting embrace of your capabilities.

Belief is your cozy quilt in the storm of doubts.

Ambition

AMBITION IS THE COMPASS of your aspirations, the magnetic pull toward your dreams. Picture ambition not as a distant mountain but as a series of peaks, each climb revealing new horizons. It is the drive that turns lofty goals into achievable milestones.

In the landscape of ambition, resilience is your hiking boots. Tread through challenges, traverse rough terrains, and let ambition be the adventure that leads you to breathtaking vistas.

So, lace up your boots, breathe in the mountain air, and let ambition be the trailblazer in the wilderness of your goals. Your ambition is not just a journey; it is the scenic route to your aspirations.

Think of ambition as your roadmap to the mountaintop moments.

Wisdom

Allow wisdom to guide your decisions. This is a word my grandma, Gloria Pershard, drilled into my head. "Be wise Tyty," she would say. Picture wisdom not as a destination but as a constant companion, whispering insights as you navigate life's twists and turns. It is the art of turning experiences into valuable knowledge.

In the mosaic of wisdom, reflection is your brush. Take moments to ponder, learn from both successes and mistakes and let wisdom be the masterpiece that paints the canvas of your choices.

So, paint your path with thoughtful strokes, and let wisdom be the guiding star in the constellation of your journey. Your wisdom is not just knowledge; it is the map leading to a more profound understanding.

"All you need to do is just relax and take your time 'pop, you will make it" -Grandma G

Strength

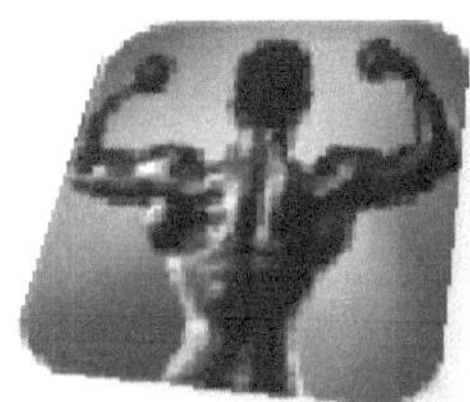

Strength is the unwavering pillar, the unyielding force that keeps you standing tall. Envision strength not as a show of force but as an inner fortitude, unshaken in the face of challenges. It is the quiet power that lies within, waiting to be tapped into.

In the tapestry of strength, each thread represents your endurance. Weave through difficulties, emerge more potent from setbacks, and let strength be the armor that shields you on your quest.

So, fortify your spirit, flex your muscles, and let strength be the silent hero in the story of your triumphs. Your strength is not just muscle; it is the backbone of your unwavering determination.

Let your strength be your silent hero.

Gratitude

DO YOU EVER FEEL THAT gentle breeze in the garden of your life?

That breeze is Gratitude. It is the whispering leaves of appreciation. Picture gratitude not as a mere expression but as a warm embrace, wrapping around you and everyone you encounter. It is the quiet magic that turns ordinary moments into extraordinary blessings.

In the tapestry of gratitude, every thread is a thank you. Weave through your experiences, acknowledge the beauty in simplicity, and let gratitude be the fragrant flowers that bloom in the garden of your heart.

Plant those seeds of thankfulness and watch as they grow into a garden, and let gratitude be the sweet aroma that lingers in the air of your journey. Your gratitude is not just politeness; it is the secret ingredient that adds flavor to your life.

Gratitude: Cultivating a garden of everyday magic

Fearless

"Fearless" is the daring leap into the unknown, the exhilarating feeling of spreading your wings. Envision fearlessness not as recklessness but as a courageous spirit, ready to soar beyond the limits. It is the bold attitude that transforms challenges into adventures.

In the landscape of fearlessness, each step is a bold stride. Walk through uncertainties, embrace the thrill of the unknown, and let fearlessness be the trailblazer on your journey to new horizons.

So, take the plunge, dance on the edge of your comfort zone, and let fearlessness be the anthem that echoes through the canyons of your aspirations. Your fearlessness is not just audacity; it is the wings that lift you to boundless heights.

NO FEAR! NO FEAR! -Budda Baker

Commitment

COMMITMENT IS THE SUPERHERO cape you wear in the daily battles of life, the unwavering promise to yourself. Imagine commitment not as a strict drill sergeant but as a loyal sidekick, supporting you through the quirks of your journey. It is the unspoken agreement that turns intentions into actions.

In the script of commitment, every scene is a choice. Act through challenges, roll with the plot twists, and let commitment be the hero that saves the day, one decision at a time.

So, throw on your superhero cape, be your protagonist, and let commitment be the blockbuster that keeps your story unfolding. Your commitment is not just a promise; it is the action-packed adventure of your life.

Commitment: Your superhero cape in the comedy of life.

Empathy

EMPATHY IS THE SECRET handshake of humanity, the language that connects us all. Picture empathy not as a complex algorithm but as a simple high-five, resonating through the shared experiences of joy and pain. It is the universal currency that fosters understanding.

In the dance of empathy, every step is a nod of recognition. Groove through the struggles, dance in the rain of emotions, and let empathy be the DJ spinning the tracks of connection.

So, share your high-fives, dance to the beats of compassion, and let empathy be the universal playlist that unites the rhythm of humanity. Your empathy is not just understanding; it is the dance floor of shared experiences.

Empathy: The universal high-five in the concert of connection.

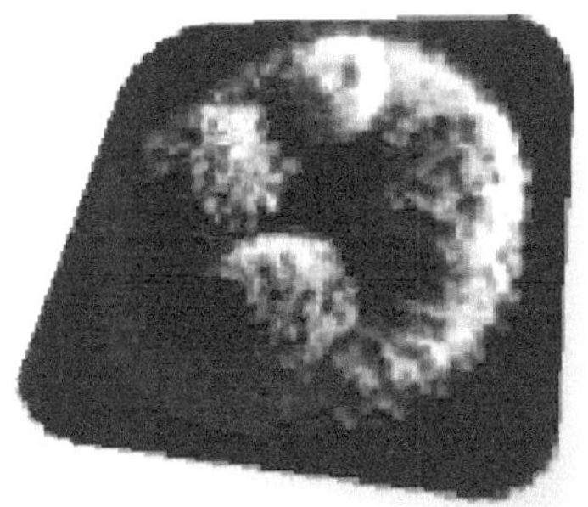

Optimism

OPTIMISM IS LIKE SEEING a positive aspect on a cloudy day; it is the positive outlook that brightens even the toughest situations. Envision optimism, not as wishful thinking, but as the mindset that sees opportunities in every difficulty. It is the belief that a cheerful outlook can make a significant impact on your life experience.

In the canvas of optimism, every stroke is a brush of hope. Paint your college journey with a cheerful perspective, celebrate small victories, and let optimism be the vibrant palette that colors your adventure.

So, put on your optimistic lens, navigate through the gray days, and let optimism be the sunshine that lights up your college path. Your optimism is not just a mindset; it is the brushstroke that adds vibrancy to your life canvas.

Optimize your endeavors and look on the bright side.

<u>Excellence</u>

Excellence is like aiming for an A+ in every assignment; it is the pursuit of academic greatness. Envision excellence not as an unattainable standard but as a commitment to giving your best effort in every academic endeavor. It is the mindset that turns routine tasks into opportunities for outstanding achievement.

In the pursuit of excellence, every project is a chance to display your capabilities. Dive into research, polish your presentations, and let excellence be the driving force that propels you toward success.

So, strive for excellence in every task, embrace the challenges, and let excellence be the guiding star that illuminates your academic journey. Your excellence is not just a grade; it is the commitment to continuously elevate your performance.

Strive for excellence.

Mindfulness

MIND·FUL·NESS

/ˈmīn(d)f(ə)lnəs/

noun

1. the quality or state of being conscious or aware of something.
2. a mental state achieved by focusing one's awareness on the present moment, while calmly acknowledging and accepting one's feelings, thoughts, and bodily sensations, used as a therapeutic technique.

Mindfulness is like focusing on one lecture at a time; it is the practice that enhances your awareness in the present moment. Picture mindfulness not as a complex concept but as the simple act of tuning into your current experience.

It is a tool that helps you navigate the academic whirlwind with clarity and intention.

In the practice of mindfulness, every breath is an anchor to the present. Inhale the knowledge, exhale the stress, and let mindfulness be the compass that guides you through the overwhelming journey of college life.

So, take a mindful pause, center yourself amidst the chaos, and let mindfulness be the steady rhythm that transforms your academic experience into a mindful exploration. Your mindfulness is not just practice; it is a gentle reminder to savor every aspect of your college journey.

Mindfully navigating through this world of chaos.

<u>Self-love</u>

SELF-LOVE IS LIKE CULTIVATING a positive relationship with yourself; it is the foundation for a healthy and fulfilling college experience. Picture self-love not as selfishness but as the practice of treating yourself with kindness and understanding. It is the mindset that fosters resilience in the face of challenges and celebrates personal victories, big or small.

In the garden of self-love, every care is a seed planted. Nurture your well-being, water the roots of your ambitions, and let self-love be the blossoming flower that adds vibrancy to your college journey.

Embrace self-love as an essential part of your college toolkit, acknowledging your worth, and let it be the empowering force that transforms challenges into opportunities for personal growth. Your self-love is not just a sentiment; it is the empowering anthem that echoes through every chapter of your academic adventure.

Self-love is the 2nd best love!

Discipline

Discipline is like crafting a structured study routine; it is the key to maintaining academic consistency. Envision discipline not as a rigid set of rules but as the intentional framework that allows you to balance academic and personal well-being. It is the mindset that turns aspirations into achievable goals through consistent effort.

In the practice of discipline, every routine is a step towards success. Set clear objectives, follow your academic schedule, and let discipline be the compass that steers you toward academic excellence.

Embrace discipline as your strategic ally on the academic battlefield, recognizing its power to transform your goals into tangible achievements. Your discipline is not just a routine; it is the secret weapon that empowers you to conquer challenges with strategic precision.

Discipline: Crafting success through intentional routines

Innovation

INNOVATION IS LIKE embracing the creativity that flows through you; it is the recognition of divine inspiration in every intellectual pursuit. Envision innovation not as a solo endeavor but as a collaborative dance with the divine. It is the acknowledgment that, in the tapestry of ideas, there is a touch of something greater guiding your unique contributions.

In the symphony of innovation, every note is a melody whispered by divine inspiration. Harmonize your thoughts, explore new horizons, and let innovation be the creative expression that echoes the divine spark within you.

Welcome innovation as a divine gift, allowing it to unfold in your academic journey, and let it be the transformative force that adds a touch of the divine to your exploration of knowledge. Your innovation is not just intellectual; it is a divine dance with the mysteries of understanding.

Innovation: Dancing with the divine in a symphony of ideas.

Balance

BALANCE IS LIKE FINDING harmony in the rhythm of your academic and personal life; it is the divine choreography that aligns your priorities. Envision balance not as a juggling act but as a dance guided by the divine, synchronizing your studies and well-being. It is the acknowledgment that, in the divine plan, your equilibrium leads to a more fulfilling life experience.

In the dance of balance, every step is a divine arrangement of priorities. Sway through your responsibilities, pirouette through moments of self-care, and let balance be the choreography that shapes your academic journey.

Embrace balance as divine guidance, recognizing the sacred flow between academics and personal growth, and let it be the celestial dance that turns your life experience into a harmonious symphony. Your balance is not just a routine; it is a divine choreography of your flourishing.

Balance is key! Remember that!

Transformation

TRANSFORMATION IS LIKE witnessing the beautiful evolution within yourself; it is a journey guided by purpose. Envision transformation not as a simple change but as a profound adventure, shaped by experiences and lessons that contribute to your growth. It is the understanding that challenges are opportunities, and each step transforms you into a more enlightened version of yourself.

In the journey of transformation, every experience is a revelation. Navigate through life's trials, embrace the lessons, and let transformation be the sculptor that shapes your character on this incredible journey.

Welcome transformation as an integral part of your life story, recognize the higher purpose in every challenge and let it be the profound metamorphosis that molds you into a masterpiece of growth. Your transformation is not just change; it is an ongoing masterpiece in the making.

Transform and embrace the beautiful evolution within.

<u>Patience</u>

PATIENCE IS LIKE TRUSTING in the natural flow of your life's journey; it is an acceptance of the unfolding events. Envision patience not as passive waiting but as a serene acceptance of the gradual progress of your unique story. It is the acknowledgment that every challenge and triumph contributes to the larger narrative of your life.

In the tapestry of patience, every thread is woven by the hand of time. Navigate through the seasons of life, allowing the natural flow to reveal your path, and let patience be the peaceful assurance that your journey is unfolding in its own perfect time.

Embrace patience as a virtue, recognizing that each moment contributes to the narrative of your story, and let it be the tranquil river that carries you through the ebb and flow of your life's exploration. Your patience is not just waiting; it is an act of trust in the unfolding chapters of your story.

Patience produces perseverance...

Inspiration

INSPIRATION IS LIKE discovering a spark within yourself; it is the catalyst for your creative journey. Envision inspiration not as a fleeting moment but as an ever-present flame, ready to ignite your passions. It is the recognition that within you lies the potential for endless creativity and the power to turn dreams into reality.

In the symphony of inspiration, every idea is a harmonious note played by the orchestra of your imagination. Dive into your creative pursuits, celebrate the birth of new ideas, and let inspiration be the driving force that fuels your journey of self-expression.

Welcome inspiration as a constant companion on your life's stage, recognizing its power to spark creativity and light the path to your dreams. Your inspiration is not just a fleeting feeling; it is the perpetual flame that illuminates your creative journey.

Inspiration: Igniting the flame of creativity within.

Generosity

Generosity is like sharing the warmth of your heart; it is kindness that creates a ripple effect in the world around you. Envision generosity not as a grand gesture but as the small, daily acts that make a big difference. It is the understanding that your kindness has the power to touch lives and create a positive impact.

In the tapestry of generosity, every act is a thread weaving a fabric of compassion. Share your kindness, extend a helping hand, and let generosity be the heartwarming force that shapes a more compassionate and connected world.

Embrace generosity as a guiding principle in your interactions, recognizing the profound effect your kindness can have on others. Your generosity is not just a gesture; it is the gentle breeze that spreads warmth and kindness wherever it goes.

Generosity takes you a long way.

Clarity

CLARITY IS LIKE OPENING a window to let the sunshine in; it is the clear vision that guides your decisions. Envision clarity not as a distant concept but as the steady illumination that dispels confusion. It is the understanding that, with a clear mind, you can navigate life's journey with purpose and direction.

In the landscape of clarity, every thought is a beacon lighting up your path. Embrace mental clarity, gain insights, and let clarity be the guiding light that brightens your decision-making process.

Welcome clarity as a trusted companion in your daily reflections, recognizing its power to bring focus to your goals. Your clarity is not just a thought; it is the guiding star that leads you toward a purposeful and enlightened journey.

Clarity: Illuminating the path to purposeful decisions.

Accountability

ACCOUNTABILITY IS LIKE being the author of your story; it is the responsibility that empowers you to shape your narrative. Envision accountability not as a burden but as the pen that writes the chapters of your life. It is the recognition that, with accountability, you have the power to take charge of your actions and influence the plot of your journey.

In the story of accountability, every choice is a sentence contributing to your character's development. Embrace responsibility, make mindful decisions, and let accountability be the narrative force that turns your aspirations into achievements.

Welcome accountability as a storytelling tool, recognizing its power to transform your goals into a compelling life story. Your accountability is not just a duty; it is the narrative arc that propels you forward in your journey.

Hold yourself accountable...

Integrity

INTEGRITY IS LIKE BUILDING a solid foundation for your character; it is consistency that defines your ethical compass. Envision integrity not as a rigid rule but as the moral compass that guides your decisions. It is the understanding that, with integrity, you create a foundation of trust and authenticity in your relationships and endeavors.

In the structure of integrity, every action is a brick fortifying the walls of your character. Uphold your principles, act with honesty, and let integrity be the cornerstone that shapes your reputation and interactions.

Welcome integrity as a timeless value, recognizing its power to foster trust and genuine connections. Your integrity is not just a virtue; it is the architectural design that builds a sturdy and trustworthy character.

Integrity: Building trust with every brick of honesty.

Joy

JOY IS LIKE SAVORING a sweet moment; it is the delightful essence that adds flavor to your experiences. Envision joy not as a fleeting emotion but as the state of being that colors your perception. It is the understanding that, with joy, you can find beauty in the simplest of moments and navigate challenges with a positive spirit.

In the canvas of joy, every smile is a stroke creating a masterpiece of contentment. Embrace the small joys, celebrate achievements, and let joy be the vibrant palette that paints your life with happiness.

Welcome joy as a constant companion, recognizing its power to transform ordinary moments into extraordinary memories. Your joy is not just an emotion; it is the artistry that adds a touch of brightness to your life's canvas.

"I got that joy joy joy joy running in my heart..." -songwriter

Harmony

HARMONY IS LIKE COMPOSING a symphony of balance; it is the integration of diverse elements into a unified melody. Envision harmony not as a complex arrangement but as the natural flow that brings equilibrium to your life. It is the understanding that, with harmony, you can create a peaceful and balanced existence.

In the symphony of harmony, every note is a representation of the various aspects of your life in perfect unison. Embrace balance, synchronize responsibilities, and let harmony be the beautiful composition that orchestrates your daily life.

Welcome harmony as a guiding principle, recognizing its power to create a melodious rhythm in your actions and relationships. Your harmony is not just a concept; it is the musical arrangement that transforms chaos into a soothing melody.

Harmonize your life.

<u>Authenticity</u>

AUTHENTICITY IS LIKE embracing your unique melody; it is the genuine expression of your true self. Envision authenticity not as conformity but as the courage to let your individuality shine. It is the understanding that, with authenticity, you can foster deeper connections and find fulfillment in being true to who you are.

In the melody of authenticity, every note is a representation of your genuine self. Embrace your uniqueness, share your story, and let authenticity be the empowering tune that resonates with those around you.

Welcome authenticity as a liberating force, recognizing its power to cultivate meaningful connections and genuine relationships. Your authenticity is not just a trait; it is the heartfelt melody that creates harmony in the composition of your life.

Authenticity: Playing your unique melody in the symphony of existence.

Radiance

RADIANCE IS LIKE LETTING your inner light shine; it is the glow that emanates from genuine positivity. Picture radiance not as an external force but as the warmth that comes from within. It is the understanding that, with radiance, you can brighten your path and inspire those around you.

In the glow of radiance, every smile is a spark illuminating your journey. Embrace positivity, share your light, and let radiance be the contagious energy that lights up your world.

Welcome radiance as a natural expression, recognizing its power to create a positive ripple effect in your life. Your radiance is not just a glow; it is the infectious brightness that lights up the darkest corners of your journey.

Sparkling from within, lighting up the world. Radiance.

Abundance

ABUNDANCE IS LIKE RECOGNIZING the wealth of everyday blessings; it is gratitude that transforms ordinary moments into treasures. Envision abundance not as an accumulation of possessions but as an appreciation for the richness of life. It is the understanding that, with an abundance mindset, you can attract positivity and prosperity.

In the richness of abundance, every moment is a gem in the treasure chest of your experiences. Embrace gratitude, savor the small joys, and let abundance be the magnet that attracts more blessings into your life.

Welcome abundance as a mindset, recognizing its power to create a life filled with fulfillment and joy. Your abundance is not just material; it is the treasure trove of gratitude that enriches your journey.

Abundance: Treasuring the riches in every moment.

Serenity

Serenity is like finding peace amid life's storms; it is the calm that soothes your soul. Envision serenity not as an escape but as the quiet strength that helps you navigate challenges with grace. It is the understanding that, with serenity, you can maintain composure and clarity even in turbulent times.

In the tranquility of serenity, every breath is a moment of peace in your journey. Embrace stillness, center yourself amidst the chaos, and let serenity be the anchor that steadies your ship.

Welcome serenity as a companion on your voyage, recognizing its power to bring balance and resilience. Your serenity is not just a fleeting calm; it is the enduring peace that keeps you afloat in the ebb and flow of life's currents.

"Eventually you'll end up where you need to be, with who you're meant to be with, doing what you should be doing." - Serenity

Positivity

POSITIVITY IS LIKE choosing sunshine over clouds; it is the optimistic lens through which you view life. Picture positivity not as ignoring challenges but as the mindset that seeks solutions and silver linings. It is the understanding that, with positivity, you can transform obstacles into stepping stones.

In the radiance of positivity, every setback is a setup for a comeback. Embrace an optimistic outlook, focus on solutions, and let positivity be the catalyst that propels you forward.

Welcome positivity as a daily choice, recognizing its power to shape a brighter narrative for your journey. Your positivity is not just a mood; it is the sunrise that paints your life with hopeful hues.

Positivity: Choosing sunshine in every chapter of life.

Blessings

BLESSINGS ARE LIKE finding unexpected gifts in everyday moments; they are reminders of life's inherent goodness. Envision blessings not as rare occurrences but as the small joys that pepper your journey. It is the understanding that, with a grateful heart, you can uncover treasures in the simplest of experiences.

In the tapestry of blessings, every day is woven with threads of gratitude. Embrace the beauty in ordinary moments, count your blessings, and let gratitude be the lens that amplifies the richness of your life.

Welcome blessings as constant companions, recognizing their power to infuse joy into your days. Your blessings are not just chance occurrences; they are the intentional sparks of goodness that light up your path.

Every blessing is a major blessing! -Blessedtyl

Faith

Faith is like trusting in the unseen; it is the belief that there is a purpose beyond what meets the eye. Envision faith not as blind trust but as the inner knowing that propels you forward. It is the understanding that, with faith, you can navigate uncertainties and find strength in the face of challenges.

In the journey of faith, every step is a testament to your trust in the unfolding story. Embrace the unknown, cultivate unwavering belief, and let faith be the guiding star that lights your way through life's mysteries.

Welcome faith as a constant companion, recognizing its power to provide solace in times of uncertainty. Your faith is not just a leap into the unknown; it is the unwavering belief that transforms challenges into opportunities.

Faith: Navigating the unseen with unwavering trust.

Illumination

ILLUMINATION IS LIKE shedding light on your path; it is the awareness that dispels the shadows of doubt. Picture illumination not as an external source but as the inner spark that brightens your understanding. It is the understanding that, with self-awareness, you can make informed choices and cultivate personal growth.

In the radiance of illumination, every insight is a beacon guiding you forward. Embrace self-discovery, seek knowledge, and let illumination be the compass that leads you toward a more enlightened version of yourself.

Welcome illumination as a lifelong journey, recognizing its power to bring clarity to your choices. Your illumination is not just a fleeting moment of insight; it is the ongoing process of self-discovery that lights up your path.

Illumination: Shining light on your path of self-discovery.

Kindness

KINDNESS IS LIKE PLANTING seeds of compassion; it is the gentle touch that nurtures the human spirit. Envision kindness not as a grand gesture but as the small acts that create a ripple effect of positivity. It is the understanding that, with kindness, you can make a significant impact on the lives of others.

In the garden of kindness, every act is a bloom of compassion. Embrace empathy, spread goodwill, and let kindness be the flourishing garden that enriches your connections and community.

Welcome kindness as a daily practice, recognizing its power to create a more compassionate world. Your kindness is not just a random act; it is the intentional cultivation of a garden that blossoms with warmth and understanding.

Kill 'em with kindness!

Adventure

Adventure is like exploring the uncharted territories of your life; it is the thrill that comes from embracing the unknown. Picture adventure not as a distant dream but as the mindset that turns everyday moments into exciting escapades. It is the understanding that, with a spirit of adventure, you can discover new facets of yourself and the world around you.

In the landscape of adventure, every step is an exploration into the realms of possibility. Embrace curiosity, seek new experiences, and let adventure be the map that leads you to the undiscovered treasures of your journey.

Welcome adventure as a lifelong companion, recognizing its power to infuse excitement into your daily life. Your adventure is not just a daring escapade; it is the journey of a lifetime filled with discovery and growth.

Adventure: Unleashing excitement in every step of your journey.

Discovery

DISCOVERY IS LIKE UNCOVERING hidden gems within yourself; it is the process of self-exploration and growth. Envision discovery not as a destination but as the ongoing journey that unfolds with each experience. It is the understanding that, with a curious mind, you can continuously unearth new layers of your identity and potential.

In the expedition of discovery, every revelation is a stepping stone to self-realization. Embrace introspection, welcome challenges, and let discovery be the compass that guides you through the intricate landscapes of your personal growth.

Welcome discovery as an ever-present adventure, recognizing its power to enrich your understanding of yourself and the world. Your discovery is not just a one-time revelation; it is the dynamic journey of self-exploration that shapes the narrative of your life.

Discovery: Unveiling the treasures within, one revelation at a time.

Awakening

AWAKENING IS LIKE OPENING your eyes to a new reality; it is the process of heightened consciousness. Picture awakening not as a sudden event but as the gradual awareness that transforms your perspective. It is the understanding that, with mindfulness, you can perceive the beauty and intricacies of life more vividly.

In the dawn of awakening, every moment is a chance to see the world with fresh eyes. Embrace mindfulness, cultivate gratitude, and let awakening be the sunrise that brightens your awareness and connection to the present.

Welcome awakening as a continual unfolding, recognizing its power to bring clarity and depth to your experiences. Your awakening is not just an isolated event; it is the ongoing process of enriching your life with profound insights and awareness.

Awakening: Embracing each moment as a new beginning.

Fulfillment

FULFILLMENT IS LIKE savoring the sweetness of achievement; it is the deep satisfaction that comes from living in alignment with your values. Envision fulfillment not as a distant goal but as the harmonious state that arises when you live authentically. It is the understanding that, with purposeful living, you can create a life that resonates with your true essence.

In the realm of fulfillment, every accomplishment is a note in the symphony of a purpose-driven life. Embrace your passions, set meaningful goals, and let fulfillment be the melody that plays in the background of your everyday existence.

Welcome fulfillment as a companion on your journey, recognizing its power to infuse your life with a sense of purpose and contentment. Your fulfillment is not just an endpoint; it is the ongoing melody that accompanies your pursuit of a meaningful life.

Fulfillment: Dancing to the melody of purpose in every step.

Alignment

ALIGNMENT IS LIKE FINDING your true north; it is the congruence between your actions and your authentic self. Picture alignment not as a rigid standard but as the dynamic balance that comes from honoring your values. It is the understanding that, with self-awareness, you can navigate life's choices in a way that resonates with your core beliefs.

In the dance of alignment, every step is a conscious choice in harmony with your true self. Embrace authenticity, make decisions aligned with your values, and let alignment be the compass that guides you through the twists and turns of your journey.

Welcome alignment as a guiding principle, recognizing its power to bring a sense of coherence and purpose to your life. Your alignment is not just a destination; it is the ongoing dance that shapes your authentic and fulfilling existence.

Alignment and assignment!

Renewal

Renewal is like a breath of fresh air after a rainstorm; it is the revitalization that follows moments of challenge and growth. Envision renewal not as a mere restart but as a continuous process of rejuvenation. It is the understanding that, with resilience, you can emerge from difficulties stronger and more vibrant.

In the cycle of renewal, every setback is an opportunity for a new beginning. Embrace challenges, learn from experiences, and let renewal be the gentle rain that nourishes the garden of your personal development.

Welcome renewal as a natural part of your journey, recognizing its power to bring vitality to your spirit. Your renewal is not just bouncing back; it is the continuous blossoming of your resilience in the face of life's storms.

Renew and bloom a new refreshing rain of life.

Courageous

Courageous is like standing tall in the face of adversity; it is the boldness that arises from a resilient spirit. Picture "courageous" not as the absence of fear but as the determination to act despite it. It is the understanding that, with bravery, you can overcome obstacles and reach new heights.

In the tapestry of courage, every challenge is an opportunity to showcase your inner strength. Embrace your fears, take bold steps, and let courage be the anthem that echoes through the triumphs and trials of your journey.

Welcome courage as a defining characteristic, recognizing its power to turn challenges into stepping stones. Your courageous spirit is not just facing fears; it is the fearless embrace of your strength in the pursuit of your dreams.

Courageous: Standing tall, facing fears, and triumphing with bold steps.

Limitless

LIMITLESS IS LIKE HAVING an open sky above you; it is the boundless potential that resides within your aspirations. Envision limitless not as the absence of challenges but as the vast expanse where your dreams can soar. It is the understanding that, with an expansive mindset, you can break through self-imposed barriers and reach new horizons.

In the realm of limitless, every goal is a stepping stone toward an ever-expanding journey. Embrace possibilities, set audacious goals, and let limitless be the mindset that propels you beyond perceived boundaries.

Welcome limitless as a guiding principle, recognizing its power to unlock your full potential. Your limitless spirit is not just dreaming big; it is the continuous expansion of your capabilities and aspirations.

Limitless: Dreaming big, reaching high, and soaring beyond the sky.

Celebration

CELEBRATION IS LIKE throwing confetti on your achievements; it is the joyful acknowledgment of milestones and victories. Picture celebration not as a fleeting moment but as the ongoing festival of your journey. It is the understanding that, with gratitude, you can amplify the positive energy surrounding your accomplishments.

In the carnival of celebration, every achievement is a reason to dance and rejoice. Embrace successes, appreciate progress, and let celebration be the rhythm that infuses joy into your daily life.

Welcome celebration as a constant companion, recognizing its power to enhance your perspective on achievements big and small. Your celebration is not just a party; it is the ongoing festival that adds vibrancy to the tapestry of your accomplishments.

Celebration: Adding confetti to every step of your victorious journey.

Authenticity

Authenticity is like wearing your favorite colors with pride; it is the genuine expression of your true self. Envision authenticity not as conformity but as the courage to let your individuality shine. It is the understanding that, with authenticity, you can foster deeper connections and find fulfillment in being true to who you are.

In the melody of authenticity, every note is a representation of your genuine self. Embrace your uniqueness, share your story, and let authenticity be the empowering tune that resonates with those around you.

Welcome authenticity as a liberating force, recognizing its power to cultivate meaningful connections and genuine relationships. Your authenticity is not just a trait; it is the heartfelt melody that creates harmony in the composition of your life.

Authenticity: Playing your unique melody in the symphony of existence.

Grace

GRACE IS LIKE DANCING through life with elegance; it is the poise that comes from embracing both challenges and triumphs. Picture grace not as a delicate stance but as the fluidity that allows you to navigate the twists and turns of your journey. It is the understanding that, with a graceful spirit, you can move through life's ups and downs with beauty and resilience.

In the dance of grace, every step is an opportunity to express your inner strength and composure. Embrace challenges with poise, celebrate victories with humility, and let grace be the choreography that enhances the beauty of your journey.

Welcome grace as a guiding principle, recognizing its power to transform challenges into moments of elegance. Your grace is not just a posture; it is the dance of resilience and beauty that enriches your life's narrative.

What gives me the most hope every day is God's grace.

Visionary

VISIONARY IS LIKE SEEING possibilities where others see limitations; it is the foresight that shapes a future filled with innovation. Envision visionary not as an exclusive trait but as the mindset that allows you to dream beyond the conventional. It is the understanding that, with a forward-thinking perspective, you can create pathways to uncharted territories.

In the landscape of visionary thinking, every idea is a spark that ignites the flame of innovation. Embrace creativity, challenge the status quo, and let being visionary be the compass that guides you toward groundbreaking solutions and possibilities.

Welcome visionary thinking as a driving force, recognizing its power to transform challenges into opportunities for growth. Your visionary mindset is not just dreaming; it is the intentional pursuit of a future shaped by innovation and possibility.

Visionary: Dreaming beyond boundaries, creating tomorrow's reality.

Triumph

TRIUMPH IS LIKE STANDING at the summit after a challenging climb; it is the victory that follows perseverance and resilience. Picture triumphs not as the absence of obstacles but as the conquering spirit that prevails over adversity. It is the understanding that, with tenacity, you can turn challenges into stepping stones toward success.

In the journey of triumph, every setback is an opportunity to rise stronger and wiser. Embrace challenges, celebrate small victories, and let triumph be the anthem that echoes through the peaks and valleys of your life's expedition.

Welcome triumph as a recurring theme in your narrative, recognizing its power to transform hardships into stories of strength and victory. Your triumph is not just a moment of success; it is the ongoing saga of resilience that shapes your life's adventure.

Triumph: Conquering challenges, standing tall at life's summits.

Release

RELEASE IS LIKE UNBURDENING your shoulders after a long journey; it is the liberation that comes from letting go of what no longer serves you. Envision "release" not as a loss but as the intentional act of creating space for new beginnings. It is the understanding that, with a lightened load, you can move forward unencumbered.

In the symphony of release, every burden shed is a note of freedom. Embrace the power of letting go, unclutter your mind, and let release be the refreshing breeze that clears the path to a brighter future.

Welcome release as a transformative process, recognizing its power to open doors to unexpected opportunities. Your release is not just relinquishing; it is the deliberate act of creating room for growth and renewal.

Release: Shedding burdens, embracing the freedom within.

Acceptance

ACCEPTANCE IS LIKE finding peace in God, amid life's uncertainties; it is the serenity that comes from embracing reality as it is. Picture acceptance not as a resignation but as the empowering choice to acknowledge and work with what you have. It is the understanding that, with a heart open to reality, you can navigate challenges with resilience and grace.

In the tapestry of acceptance, every circumstance is a thread woven into the fabric of your journey. Embrace the present moment, learn from experiences, and let acceptance be the soothing melody that accompanies you through life's twists and turns.

Welcome acceptance as a powerful ally, recognizing its ability to transform hardships into opportunities for growth. Your acceptance is not just surrendering; it is the courageous act of finding strength in embracing the beauty of imperfection.

Acceptance: Embracing reality, weaving peace into every moment.

<u>Harmony</u>

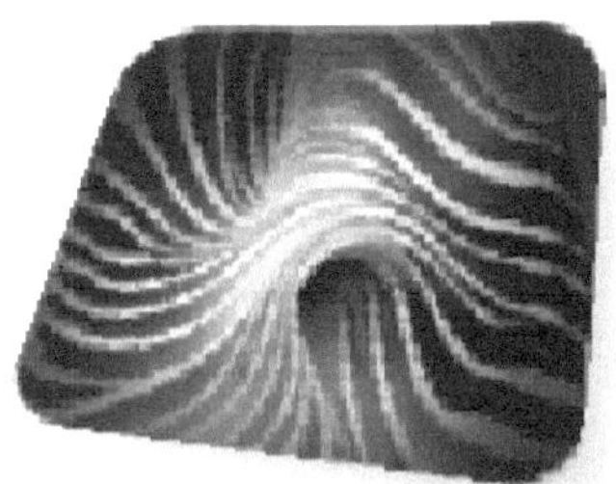

Harmony is like orchestrating a symphony of balance in your life; it is the artful integration of diverse elements into a beautiful composition. Envision harmony not as a static state but as a dynamic dance that brings equilibrium to your days. It is the understanding that, with intentional choices, you can create a melody of well-being.

In the ballet of harmony, every decision is a graceful movement contributing to the rhythm of your life. Embrace balance, adjust the tempo when needed, and let harmony be the masterpiece that resonates with peace and fulfillment.

Welcome harmony as a daily practice, recognizing its power to bring a sense of coherence to your experiences. Your harmony is not just a momentary balance; it is the ongoing choreography that turns the chaos into a symphony of tranquility.

Imagine dancing through life with a symphony of balance...
that's harmony.

Boldness

BOLDNESS IS LIKE PAINTING your canvas with vibrant strokes; it is the audacity that comes from embracing your uniqueness and taking confident strides. Picture boldness not as recklessness but as the fearless expression of your authentic self. It is the understanding that, with courage, you can turn your canvas into a masterpiece of individuality.

In the gallery of boldness, every choice is a stroke adding character and depth to your life's painting. Embrace your quirks, take risks, and let boldness be the palette that transforms your journey into a work of art.

Welcome boldness as a liberating force, recognizing its power to infuse your narrative with spontaneity and courage. Your boldness does not just stand out; it is the vibrant expression that turns the ordinary into an extraordinary masterpiece.

Boldness: Painting your journey with strokes of uniqueness.

Praise

PRAISE IS LIKE SPRINKLING joy over your accomplishments; it is the celebration that magnifies the positive energy surrounding your achievements. Picture praise, not as external validation, but as the self-appreciation that fuels your journey. It is the understanding that, with gratitude, you can amplify the brightness of your successes.

In the symphony of praise, every accomplishment is a note resonating with the melody of your progress. Embrace your victories, acknowledge your efforts, and let praise be the anthem that fills your life with a sense of accomplishment and joy.

Welcome praise as a motivating force, recognizing its power to inspire continued excellence. Your praise is not just external acknowledgment; it is the internal recognition that turns your journey into a celebration of your capabilities.

Give praises unto God, give praises.

<u>Liberation</u>

LIBERATION IS LIKE breaking free from self-imposed chains; it is emancipation that comes from embracing your autonomy and authenticity. Envision liberation not as an escape but as the empowerment that arises when you live true to yourself. It is the understanding that, with self-liberation, you can carve a path aligned with your values and aspirations.

In the journey of liberation, every step is a stride toward personal freedom. Embrace self-expression, challenge societal norms, and let liberation be the anthem that echoes through the choices you make, creating a life unbound by limitations.

Welcome liberation as a transformative force, recognizing its power to unlock your potential and redefine your narrative. Your liberation is not just breaking chains; it is the conscious choice to live boldly and authentically.

Liberation: Embracing freedom, rewriting your own story.

Radiant

RADIANCE IS LIKE LETTING your inner light illuminate your path; it is the luminosity that comes from embracing positivity and self-love. Picture radiance not as a fleeting glow but as the enduring brightness that emanates from your authentic self. It is the understanding that, with self-care, you can shine brightly even in the face of challenges.

In the brilliance of radiance, every smile reflects your inner joy. Embrace self-love, radiate positivity, and let your radiance be the beacon that guides you through life's twists and turns.

Welcome radiance as a constant companion, recognizing its power to uplift your spirits and brighten the lives of those around you. Your radiance is not just a momentary sparkle; it is the enduring light that adds warmth to your journey.

Radiant: Illuminating your path with the light of self-love.

Transcendence

TRANSCENDENCE IS LIKE soaring beyond the ordinary; it is the elevation that comes from embracing growth and expanding your horizons. Envision transcendence not as a distant ideal but as the continual evolution that propels you beyond your comfort zone. It is the understanding that, with a growth mindset, you can rise above challenges and discover new heights.

In the flight of transcendence, every lesson is a wing that helps you soar higher. Embrace personal development, learn from experiences, and let transcendence be the wind beneath your wings, carrying you toward a more elevated and enlightened existence.

Welcome transcendence as an ongoing journey, recognizing its power to transform challenges into stepping stones toward your aspirations. Your transcendence is not just a lofty goal; it is the continual ascent toward the best version of yourself.

Transcendence: Soaring beyond limits, evolving to new heights.

Unstoppable

UNSTOPPABLE IS LIKE a force that propels you forward; it is the determination that arises from resilience and an unwavering spirit. Picture being unstoppable not as a lack of challenges but as the commitment to press on despite them. It is the understanding that, with tenacity, you can turn obstacles into opportunities.

In the journey of being unstoppable, every setback is a stepping stone toward greater strength. Embrace challenges, persevere through difficulties, and let being unstoppable be the driving force that propels you toward your goals and dreams.

Welcome being unstoppable as a defining characteristic, recognizing its power to turn adversity into triumph. Your unstoppable spirit is not just enduring challenges; it is the fierce determination that shapes your narrative into a story of resilience and victory.

Cannot stop the unstoppable.

Revitalization

REVITALIZATION IS LIKE a breath of fresh air for your spirit; it is the renewal that comes from embracing change and welcoming new energy into your life. Envision revitalization not as a reaction to stagnation but as a proactive choice to invigorate your mind, body, and soul. It is the understanding that, with a rejuvenated perspective, you can breathe life into every facet of your existence.

In the landscape of revitalization, every moment of change is a seed planted for growth. Embrace transformation, open yourself to new possibilities, and let revitalization be the breeze that carries away the old, making space for the new.

Welcome revitalization as an intentional act, recognizing its power to infuse your journey with a sense of aliveness. Your revitalization is not just reacting to life; it is the conscious decision to embrace each day with renewed vigor.

Revitalization: Breathing new life into every moment.

Invigoration

INVIGORATION IS LIKE a surge of energy coursing through your veins; it is the lively spirit that comes from embracing enthusiasm and embracing the vitality of life. Picture invigoration not as a fleeting burst but as an ongoing dance with the rhythm of your passions. It is the understanding that, with an invigorated heart, you can infuse your journey with a sense of purpose and dynamism.

In the dance of invigoration, every endeavor is a step toward a more vibrant and fulfilling life. Embrace your passions, fuel your ambitions, and let invigoration be the heartbeat that propels you toward a life brimming with energy and zest.

Welcome invigoration as a constant companion, recognizing its power to turn routine into an exciting adventure. Your invigoration is not just a momentary spark; it is the ongoing rhythm that animates your journey.

Invigoration: Dancing through life with a heart full of vitality.

Endurance

ENDURANCE IS LIKE A steadfast anchor during life's storms; it is the resilience that comes from embracing challenges with unwavering strength. Picture endurance, not as passive resistance, but as the unyielding commitment to weather any storm that comes your way. It is the understanding that, with a tenacious spirit, you can persist through difficulties and emerge stronger.

In the landscape of endurance, every trial is a testament to your inner strength. Embrace adversity, cultivate resilience, and let endurance be the lighthouse that guides you through the darkest nights, illuminating a path to triumph.

Welcome endurance as an enduring companion, recognizing its power to transform hardships into stepping stones toward your aspirations. Your endurance is not just surviving challenges; it is the indomitable spirit that shapes your journey into a story of triumph.

Endurance: Navigating storms with an unyielding spirit.

Prowess

PROWESS IS LIKE SKILLFUL navigation through life's challenges; it is the mastery that comes from embracing your strengths and talents. Envision prowess not as a display of superiority but as a humble recognition of your unique abilities. It is the understanding that, with honed skills, you can chart a course towards your goals with confidence and expertise.

In the journey of prowess, every obstacle is an opportunity to display your capabilities. Embrace continuous learning, refine your skills, and let prowess be the compass that guides you through uncharted territories, transforming challenges into triumphs.

Welcome prowess as a continual journey, recognizing its power to unlock your potential and shape your narrative. Your prowess is not just a showcase of talents; it is the dynamic force that propels you towards excellence.

Prowess: Navigating life's challenges with skillful mastery.

Zeal

ZEAL IS LIKE A FIERY passion that fuels your journey; it is the intense enthusiasm that comes from embracing your pursuits with unwavering energy. Picture zeal not as a fleeting emotion but as the perpetual flame that burns within, propelling you forward with purpose and determination. It is the understanding that, with a fervent heart, you can infuse your endeavors with a contagious energy.

In the blaze of zeal, every endeavor is an opportunity to pour your heart and soul into what you love. Embrace passion, cultivate enthusiasm, and let zeal be the driving force that turns your dreams into vibrant realities.

Welcome zeal as an enduring fire, recognizing its power to ignite the path to your aspirations. Your zeal is not just a momentary burst; it is the perpetual flame that brightens your journey and inspires those around you.

Zeal: Fueling the journey with unwavering passion.

<u>Boundless</u>

BOUNDLESS IS LIKE THE vast expanse of the sky; it is the limitless potential that comes from embracing an open mind and expansive possibilities. Picture boundless not as an abstract concept but as the dynamic space where your dreams and ambitions soar freely. It is the understanding that, with an open heart, you can break free from limitations and embrace a life without boundaries.

In the canvas of boundless, every dream is a brushstroke painting the picture of your expansive aspirations. Embrace creativity, welcome new horizons, and let boundless be the canvas that invites you to explore the vastness of your potential.

Welcome boundless as an expansive mindset, recognizing its power to transform your perception of what is achievable. Your boundless spirit is not just dreaming; it is the constant invitation to explore the limitless possibilities that await.

Boundless: Painting your dreams on the canvas of endless possibilities.

Unity

UNITY IS LIKE A HARMONIOUS melody of diversity; it is the collective strength that comes from embracing the richness of different voices and perspectives. Picture unity not as conformity but as a celebration of the unique contributions everyone brings. It is the understanding that, with a collaborative spirit, you can create a symphony where every note adds to the beauty of the whole.

In the orchestra of unity, every person is an essential instrument playing a distinct role. Embrace diversity, foster inclusion, and let unity be the guiding rhythm that transforms discord into a harmonious ensemble.

Welcome unity as a powerful force, recognizing its ability to create positive change and amplify the impact of collective efforts. Your unity is not just coming together; it is the harmonious collaboration that creates a world of shared dreams and aspirations.

Everyone needs somebody. UNITE!

Momentum

MOMENTUM IS LIKE A surge of energy propelling you forward; it is the dynamic force that comes from embracing progress and maintaining a steady rhythm of action. Envision momentum not as a fleeting push but as a consistent flow that builds with each step you take. It is the understanding that, with a determined spirit, you can turn inertia into a powerful force driving you towards your goals.

In the journey of momentum, every small action is a building block contributing to the acceleration of your endeavors. Embrace consistency, celebrate progress, and let momentum be the tailwind that carries you through challenges, transforming obstacles into stepping stones.

Welcome momentum as a guiding force, recognizing its power to turn aspirations into achievements. Your momentum is not just a burst of energy; it is the ongoing flow that transforms your journey into a dynamic adventure.

Momentum: Turning dreams into a powerful force of action.

Wholeness

WHOLENESS IS LIKE COMPLETING a puzzle with your authentic pieces; it is the completeness that comes from embracing every aspect of yourself. Envision wholeness not as perfection but as a journey of self-acceptance and integration. It is the understanding that, with self-love, you can embrace your strengths and imperfections, creating a mosaic of authenticity.

In the mosaic of wholeness, every experience is a piece that contributes to the beautiful tapestry of your life. Embrace self-discovery, celebrate your uniqueness, and let wholeness be the canvas where you paint the story of your evolving, authentic self.

Welcome wholeness as a continuous process, recognizing its power to transform self-doubt into self-love. Your wholeness is not just a destination; it is the ongoing masterpiece that unfolds with each moment of acceptance. TRUST GOD!

Wholeness: Creating a masterpiece with the pieces of your authentic self.

Prosperity

PROSPERITY IS LIKE a garden in full bloom; it is the abundant growth that comes from embracing a mindset of abundance and gratitude. Envision prosperity not as a mere accumulation of wealth but as a holistic abundance in every area of your life. It is the understanding that, with gratitude, you can cultivate a garden where success, well-being, and fulfillment flourish.

In the garden of prosperity, every seed of gratitude is a promise of bountiful harvests. Embrace abundance, nurture positive thoughts, and let prosperity be the fertile soil in which your dreams take root and flourish.

Welcome prosperity as a holistic state, recognizing its power to enrich your life in various dimensions. Your prosperity is not just financial success; it is the garden where every aspect of your life blooms with fulfillment and joy.

Prosperity: Cultivating a garden of abundance with a heart full of gratitude.

<u>Laughter</u>

LAUGHTER IS LIKE A melody that brings joy to your soul; it is the lightness that comes from embracing humor and finding delight in life's moments. Picture laughter not as a response to external events but as an internal choice to see the lighter side of things. It is the understanding that, with a joyful spirit, you can transform challenges into opportunities for amusement.

In the melody of laughter, every chuckle is a note adding to the symphony of your happiness. Embrace playfulness, share moments of joy, and let laughter be the soundtrack that accompanies you through life, turning ordinary moments into extraordinary memories.

Welcome laughter as a source of resilience, recognizing its power to uplift your spirit and create bonds with others. Your laughter is not just a reaction; it is the intentional choice to infuse your journey with joy.

Laughter: Creating a symphony of joy in life's delightful moments.

Charismatic

CHARISMATIC IS LIKE a magnetic feeling that captivates hearts; it is the enchanting energy that comes from embracing authenticity and radiating positive charisma. Envision charisma not as a performance but as a genuine expression of your vibrant personality. It is the understanding that, with authenticity, you can leave a lasting impression on those around you.

In the charm of charismatic energy, every genuine connection is a thread weaving a tapestry of positive influence. Embrace authenticity, celebrate your uniqueness, and let charisma be the magnetic force that draws people to your light, creating a harmonious dance of connections.

Welcome charisma as a natural extension of your true self, recognizing its power to create a positive ripple effect in your interactions. Your charisma is not just about surface charm; it is the authentic radiance that leaves an indelible mark on the hearts of others.

Be yourself, like Charisma!

Clever

BEING CLEVER IS LIKE having a dependable sidekick in your journey; it's the smart approach that comes from embracing wit and creative problem-solving. Imagine cleverness not as a daunting puzzle but as a friendly companion helping you navigate life's challenges. It is the understanding that, with a quick mind, you can turn obstacles into opportunities for growth and laughter.

In the realm of cleverness, every witty solution is like a high-five from your ingenious sidekick. Embrace creativity, enjoy the process of finding solutions, and let cleverness be the trusty ally that adds a sprinkle of fun to your daily adventures.

Welcome cleverness as a down-to-earth friend, recognizing its power to make your journey smoother and more enjoyable. Your cleverness is not just about intellect; it is the practical wisdom that turns everyday situations into moments of triumph.

Proverbs 14:8-19: Why is a clever person wise? Because he knows what to do.

Colossal

FEELING COLOSSAL IS like having a superhero moment in your own story; it is the powerful energy that comes from thanking God for your strengths and impact. Picture feeling colossal not as an overwhelming responsibility but as an empowering realization of your potential. It is the understanding that, with confidence, you can make a significant difference in your own life and the lives of others.

In the world of feeling colossal, every achievement is like a superhero cape fluttering in the wind. Embrace your strengths, celebrate your victories, and let that colossal feeling be the source of inspiration that propels you forward, turning aspirations into achievements.

Welcome the colossal feeling as an empowering force, recognizing its power to fuel your determination and inspire those around you. Your colossal feeling is not just about personal success; it is the superhero within you making a positive impact on the world.

Colossal: Embracing your superhero moment in the story of life.

Create

CREATING IS LIKE CO-laboring with the Creator; it is the intentional act that comes from embracing the divine inspiration and creativity bestowed upon you. Picture creation not as a solitary endeavor but as a partnership with God, the ultimate Artist. It is the understanding that, with a heart tuned to His wisdom, you can bring beauty into the world.

In the canvas of creation, every stroke is a collaboration with the divine hands that shaped the universe. Embrace inspiration, seek divine guidance, and let your creativity be the harmonious dance with God's plan, turning your endeavors into a masterpiece reflecting His glory.

Welcome creating as an act of worship, recognizing its power to reflect the divine image within you. Your creative expression is not just about personal talent; it is the co-creation that aligns your heart with the Creator.

Have "Jesus-like" creativity.

Dedicated

BEING DEDICATED IS like tending to a garden of dreams; it is the committed effort that comes from embracing perseverance and working towards your goals. Imagine dedication not as a burdensome task but as a loving care for the seeds of your aspirations. It is the understanding that, with unwavering commitment, you can nurture your dreams into flourishing realities.

In the garden of dedication, every consistent action is like sunlight and water, encouraging the growth of your ambitions. Embrace resilience, stay focused on your objectives, and let dedication be the nurturing force that transforms your aspirations into a blooming garden of achievements.

Welcome dedication as a loving gardener, recognizing its power to cultivate a future rich with the fruits of your hard work. Your dedication is not just about the result; it is the daily act of caring for your dreams and watching them blossom.

Dedicated: Cultivating a garden of dreams with unwavering care.

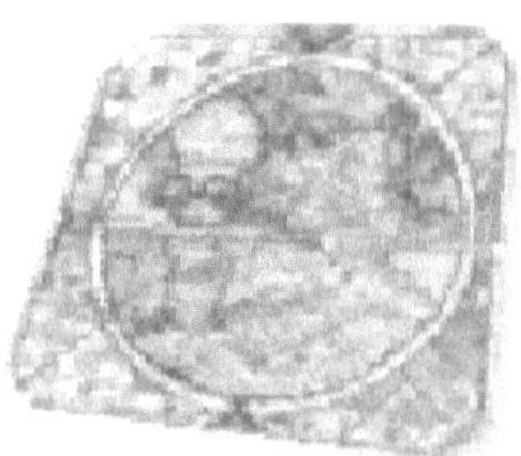

Deliberate

BEING DELIBERATE IS like crafting a roadmap for your journey; it is the planning that comes from embracing mindfulness and thoughtful decision-making. Picture deliberation, not as a slow process, but as a purposeful choice to shape your path. It is the understanding that, with conscious decisions, you can navigate your life with clarity and purpose.

In the art of deliberation, every thoughtful choice is like a milestone guiding you toward your desired destination. Embrace mindfulness, take intentional actions, and let deliberation be the compass that ensures each step aligns with your values, turning the chaotic into the organized.

Welcome deliberation as a strategic ally, recognizing its power to bring focus and direction to your endeavors. Your deliberation is not just about overthinking; it is the thoughtful approach that transforms uncertainty into a well-orchestrated symphony of your life.

Deliberate: Crafting a purposeful roadmap for your life's journey

Delight

EXPERIENCING DELIGHT is like savoring the sweetness of life; it is the joyful appreciation that comes from embracing moments of happiness and gratitude. Imagine delight not as a fleeting emotion but as a conscious choice to find joy in simple pleasures. It is the understanding that, with a heart full of appreciation, you can turn mundane moments into delightful memories.

In the feast of delight, every small joy is like a delectable treat adding flavor to the banquet of your experiences. Embrace gratitude, savor the sweetness of the present, and let delight be the seasoning that enhances the richness of your everyday life, turning the ordinary into the extraordinary.

Welcome "delight" as a cherished friend, recognizing its power to brighten your days and uplift your spirit. Your delight is not just about the grand moments; it is the intentional act of finding joy in the small, magical details of life.

Delight: Savoring the sweetness of life's delightful moments.

Devoted

BEING DEVOTED IS LIKE nurturing the flame of your passions; it is the loyal commitment that comes from embracing what you love and investing your energy in meaningful pursuits. Imagine devotion not as a sacrifice but as a joyous act of dedicating yourself to what brings you fulfillment. It is the understanding that, with wholehearted commitment, you can create a life rich with purpose and satisfaction.

In the realm of devotion, every dedicated moment is like adding fuel to the fire of your passions. Embrace what you love, invest your time in meaningful activities, and let devotion be the warm glow that illuminates your journey, turning ordinary days into extraordinary expressions of your true self.

Welcome devotion as a source of inspiration, recognizing its power to ignite your enthusiasm and fuel your creativity. Your devotion is not just about the tasks at hand; it is the intentional choice to infuse your life with the warmth of purpose.

Devoted: Nurturing the flame of passions with wholehearted commitment.

Dream

TO DREAM IS LIKE HAVING a personal compass that guides you toward your aspirations; it is the imaginative vision that comes from embracing hope and envisioning a future filled with possibilities. Picture dreaming not as a mere fantasy but as a powerful force that fuels your journey. It is the understanding that, with a hopeful heart, you can turn your ambitions into tangible realities.

In the landscape of dreams, every goal is like a destination on the map of your desires. Embrace optimism, set bold intentions, and let dreaming be the compass that propels you forward, turning aspirations into achievements.

Welcome dreams as the architects of your reality, recognizing their power to shape your journey and inspire you to reach new heights. Your dreams are not just wishful thinking; they're the blueprints that lead you toward a future filled with purpose and fulfillment.

"I had a dream..."

<u>Driven</u>

BEING DRIVEN IS LIKE having a powerful engine that propels you forward in your endeavors; it is the determined energy that comes from embracing ambition and staying focused on your goals. Picture being driven not as a relentless pursuit but as an enthusiastic journey toward your desired destination. It is the understanding that, with fiery determination, you can navigate challenges and make progress even in the face of obstacles.

In the engine of being driven, every action is like a powerful thrust propelling you closer to your ambitions. Embrace perseverance, stay committed to your objectives, and let being driven by the force that accelerates your journey, turn setbacks into stepping stones.

Welcome being driven as a dynamic force, recognizing its power to keep your momentum strong and infuse your path with resilience. Your drive is not just about reaching the destination; it is the relentless pursuit of growth and achievement.

Driven: Fueling your journey with the powerful engine of ambition.

Ease

TO EMBRACE EASE IS like navigating through life with a gentle breeze at your back; it is the harmonious flow that comes from embracing simplicity and finding peace within. Picture ease not as a luxury but as an intentional choice to approach life with a light heart. It is the understanding that, with a calm spirit, you can navigate challenges and savor the beauty of each moment through the grace of God.

In the realm of ease, every breath is like a soothing melody, guiding you through the symphony of your experiences. Embrace simplicity, release unnecessary burdens, and let ease be the gentle companion that accompanies you on your journey, turning complexities into moments of graceful navigation.

Welcome "ease" as a calming force, recognizing its power to bring balance and serenity to your endeavors. Your embrace of ease is not just about avoiding difficulties; it is the intentional decision to dance through life with the lightness of being.

Ease: Navigating life's symphony with a gentle breeze of simplicity.

Effortless

BEING EFFORTLESS IS like a dance where every step feels natural and free; it is the fluid grace that comes from embracing your strengths and allowing things to unfold with ease. Picture effortlessness not as a lack of engagement but as a state of natural flow where your authentic self shines. It is the understanding that, with authenticity, you can accomplish tasks with grace and make progress without unnecessary strain.

In the dance of effortlessness, every action is like a seamless movement, expressing the beauty of your capabilities. Embrace your strengths, trust your instincts, and let effortlessness be the dance partner that accompanies you, turning challenges into moments of elegant navigation.

Welcome effortlessness as a harmonious presence, recognizing its power to infuse your actions with grace and efficiency. Your embrace of effortlessness is not about avoiding challenges; it is the art of navigating them with a sense of natural flow.

Effortless: Dancing through challenges with the grace of authenticity.

Elevated

FEELING ELEVATED IS like soaring to new heights in the sky of your achievements; it is the uplifting energy that comes from embracing success and recognizing your progress. Picture elevation not as a distant peak but as a continuous ascent, one step at a time. It is the understanding that, with each accomplishment, you can reach new altitudes and expand the horizons of what is possible.

In the journey of elevation, every step forward is like a triumph that propels you higher in the sky of your aspirations. Embrace success, celebrate your victories, and let elevation be the wind beneath your wings, turning challenges into opportunities to soar.

Welcome elevation as a constant companion, recognizing its power to lift your spirit and inspire you to reach for the stars. Your sense of elevation is not just about reaching the summit; it is the continuous ascent that allows you to explore new vistas and embrace the beauty of your journey.

Elevated: Soaring to new heights in the sky of your achievements.

<u>Enrich</u>

TO ENRICH IS LIKE INFUSING your life with the valuable nutrients of wisdom and experiences; it is the conscious act that comes from embracing growth and recognizing the lessons within each moment. Picture enrichment, not as a passive accumulation, but as an intentional process of refining your understanding. It is the understanding that, with an open mind, you can turn every experience into an opportunity for learning and personal development.

In the journey of enrichment, every lesson is like a precious gem, adding brilliance to the tapestry of your life. Embrace curiosity, seek knowledge, and let enrichment be the steady flow that nourishes your mind and soul, turning challenges into stepping stones to wisdom.

Welcome enrichment as a lifelong companion, recognizing its power to make your journey a rich and fulfilling adventure. Your enrichment is not just about gaining knowledge; it is the active pursuit of wisdom that adds depth and meaning to your existence.

Enrich: Nourishing the tapestry of your life with the gems of wisdom.

Epic

FEELING EPIC IS LIKE living in a blockbuster movie where every day is an adventure; it is the thrilling energy that comes from embracing excitement and turning ordinary moments into extraordinary tales. Picture epic experiences not as grand events but as the accumulation of small, joyful victories. It is the understanding that, with a zest for life, you can transform routine activities into scenes filled with energy and enthusiasm.

In the saga of epic living, every chapter is like a memorable sequence, making your life a story worth telling. Embrace excitement, find joy in the details, and let epic moments be the highlights that make your journey cinematic, turning the mundane into an adventure.

Welcome an epic mindset as a thrilling companion, recognizing its power to make your life a tale of excitement and fun. Your epic living is not just about major events; it is the intentional choice to infuse every day with the energy of a blockbuster movie.

Epic: Turning "the everyday" into an adventure, making life a blockbuster.

Exciting

THINK OF "EXCITING" as turning up the volume on your favorite song; it is the dynamic energy that comes from embracing enthusiasm and finding joy in the rhythm of your experiences. Picture excitement not as a rare emotion but as a daily beat that adds spice to your routine. It is the understanding that, with a lively spirit, you can turn even the simplest moments into occasions for celebration.

In the melody of exciting living, every beat is like a cheerful note, making your life a song worth dancing to. Embrace enthusiasm, celebrate your victories, and let exciting moments be the beats that make your journey a lively dance, turning the ordinary into a celebration.

Welcome excitement as a constant rhythm, recognizing its power to make your life a vibrant and upbeat song. Your exciting moments are not just about grand events; they are the intentional choice to groove through life with a lively and spirited dance.

Exciting: Turning the ordinary into a lively dance of joyous moments.

Fun

BEING FUN IS LIKE TURNING every day into a playful adventure; it is the lighthearted energy that comes from embracing joy and finding laughter in the simplicity of life. Picture fun, not as an occasional event, but as a spontaneous party that breaks out during your routine. It is the understanding that, with a cheerful spirit, you can turn even mundane moments into occasions for laughter and delight.

In the carnival of fun living, every moment is like a colorful attraction, making your life a joyful ride. Embrace playfulness, find humor in everyday situations, and let fun be the vibrant atmosphere that makes your journey a delightful celebration, turning the ordinary into a festival of joy.

Welcome fun as a carefree companion, recognizing its power to make your life a joyous and playful experience. Your fun moments are not just about special occasions; they are the spontaneous parties that add laughter and lightness to your daily adventure.

Fun: Turning the ordinary into a spontaneous festival of joy.

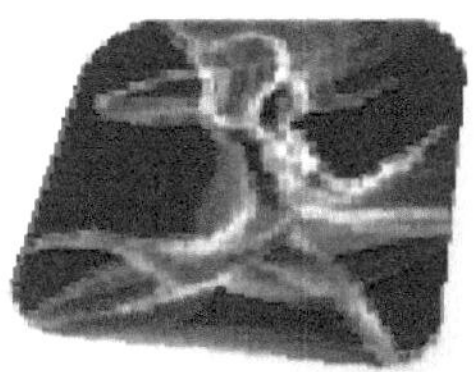

Motion

TO BE IN MOTION IS like dancing through the rhythm of life; it is the dynamic energy that comes from embracing change and recognizing the constant flow of experiences. Picture motion not as a chaotic force but as a graceful dance where each step propels you forward. It is the understanding that, with a flexible spirit, you can turn transitions into opportunities for growth and fluidity.

In the ballet of motion, every step is like a note in a lively melody, making your life a symphony of ever-evolving experiences. Embrace adaptability, welcome change, and let motion be the guiding choreography that adds grace to your journey, turning challenges into opportunities for graceful transformation.

Welcome motion as a rhythmic companion, recognizing its power to make your life a dance of continuous adaptation and fluidity. Your motion is not just about navigating uncertainties; it is the intentional choice to dance through the ups and downs, creating a harmonious rhythm in the orchestra of your life.

Motion: Turning life's transitions into a graceful dance of continuous adaptation.

Blessed

TO FEEL BLESSED IS like recognizing the abundant gifts that God has bestowed upon you; it is the gratitude-filled energy that comes from embracing the beauty in every moment. Picture feeling blessed not as a passive state, but as an active appreciation for the richness of your experiences. It is the understanding that, with a grateful heart, you can turn ordinary occurrences into sources of joy and abundance.

In the landscape of feeling blessed, every moment becomes a treasure, making your life a tapestry of gratitude. Embrace appreciation, savor the simple joys, and let feeling blessed be the gentle rain that nourishes your journey, turning challenges into opportunities for abundant growth.

Welcome the feeling of being blessed as a heartwarming companion, recognizing its power to make your life a journey of continuous appreciation and fulfillment. Your sense of being blessed is not just about acknowledging the good times; it is the intentional choice to find joy in every aspect of your existence.

Blessed: Turning life's moments into a tapestry of gratitude and abundance.

Echoes of Hope: Mapping Your Path With 100 Empowering Words
By Tylor Miller

Dear Fellow Dancer,

As you close the final page of "Echoes of Hope," I do not want to say goodbye, but rather, "until we meet again on the dance floor of life." It has been a privilege to guide you through this exploration of affirmations, gratitude, and the ever-present echo of hope within.

Thank you for taking this journey with me. Remember, the music never truly stops. The affirmations you have discovered within these pages are not mere words, but companions on your continued journey. Carry them with you, whisper them in the quiet moments, and let them resonate with the wellness of your mind.

Go forth, dear friend, and waltz with your worries, tango with your fears, and pirouette with your dreams. May your steps be light, your heart be full, and your spirit forever dance to the rhythm of hope. And always know that God is leading you along your path.

With gratitude and warm wishes,

The Author of "Echoes of Hope"

Thanks again to you all for tuning in to the sound of an echoed hope. I wish you many blessings and coverage in all human endeavors!

Tylor Miller & the E.O.H. team

SOCIALS

Connect with Tylor Miller on social media; Instagram: @blessedtyl | @echoeshope; and let the journey continue beyond the pages of "Echoes of Hope."

SCAN HERE

About the Author

Meet Tylor Miller, the creative force behind "Echoes of Hope." Born in London, England, yet raised in a single-parent household in the heart of Miami, FL, stood an inspirational soul with a passion for words that resonate like prayers.

Tylor always had a sense of entrepreneurship yet was not too clear on what avenue to pursue. All he could lean on was his love for writing since a child. He began crafting journal entries and poems that reflected his experiences, struggles, and triumphs, drawn from the rigorous environments that shaped his upbringing.

Despite facing numerous challenges along the way, including financial constraints and societal expectations, Tylor remained steadfast in his pursuit of literary expression. He drew inspiration from both classic and contemporary authors, finding solace and motivation in their words.

Tylor Miller tries his best to stand as a beacon of hope in an environment often overshadowed by negativity.